Naming Words

Nouns and Pronouns

Anita Ganeri

Raintree

www.raintreepublishers.co.uk
Visit our website to find out
more information about
Raintree books.

To order:
☎ Phone 0845 6044371
📄 Fax +44 (0) 1865 312263
📠 Email myorders@raintreepublishers.co.uk

Customers from outside the UK please telephone +44 1865 312262

Raintree is an imprint of Capstone Global Library Limited,
a company incorporated in England and Wales having its
registered office at 7 Pilgrim Street, London, EC4V 6LB
– Registered company number: 6695582

Edited by Daniel Nunn, Rebecca Rissman, and Sian Smith
Designed by Joanna Hinton-Malivoire
Picture research by Tracy Cummins
Original illustrations © Capstone Global Library
Illustrated by Joanna Hinton-Malivoire
Production by Eirian Griffiths
Originated by Capstone Global Library Ltd
Printed and bound in China by South China Printing
Company Ltd

ISBN 978 1 406 23239 4
15 14 13 12 11
10 9 8 7 6 5 4 3 2 1

British Library Cataloguing in Publication Data
Ganeri, Anita, 1961-
Naming words: nouns and pronouns. (Getting to grips
with grammar)
425.5'4-dc22
A full catalogue record for this book is available from the
British Library.

Acknowledgements
We would like to thank the following for permission to
reproduce photographs and artworks: Dreamstime.com
pp.22 (© Fotomorgana), 26 (© Annminina); istockphoto p.24
(© Linda Kloosterhof); Shutterstock pp.5 (© Greg da Silva), 6
(© Bannykh Alexey Vladimirovich), 7 (© Dmitry Naumov), 8
left (© M. Unal Ozmen), 8 right (© joingate), 9 (© p.schwarz),
10 (© Iwona Grodzka), 11 (© Kletr), 13 (© Vaclav Volrab), 14 (©
JungleOutThere), 15 (© Gorelova), 17 (© joingate), 18 (© Viorel
Sima), 19 (© Monkey Business Images), 20 (© Studio 1One), 25
(© Big Pants Production), 27 (© Cory Thoman), 28 (© i359702),
30 (© AJP).

Every effort has been made to contact copyright holders
of material reproduced in this book. Any omissions will
be rectified in subsequent printings if notice is given to the
publisher.

Contents

Some words are shown in bold, **like this**.
You can find them in the glossary on page 31.

What is grammar?

Grammar is a set of rules that helps you to write and speak a language. Grammar is important because it helps people to understand each other.

> **went Today swimming. I in the sea**

Without grammar, this **sentence** doesn't make sense.

In grammar, words are divided into different types. These are called parts of speech. They show how words are used. This book is about parts of speech called **nouns**.

Today I went swimming in the sea.

Grammar turns the jumbled-up words into a sentence.

What is a noun?

A **noun** is a naming word. A noun is used to name a person, an animal, a place, or a thing.

The dog barked at the cat.

'Dog' and 'cat' are nouns. They tell you the names of the animals.

The **boy** is riding a **bike**.

'Boy' and 'bike' are nouns. They tell you the names of someone and something.

It is easy to find out if something is a noun. If a word tells you the name of someone or something, it is a noun.

Spot the noun

Look at this list of words. Can you pick out all the **nouns** in the list? Remember that a noun is a naming word.

sandy

bucket

spade

ice cream

quickly

sandcastle

'Bucket', 'spade', 'ice cream', and 'sandcastle' are nouns. 'Sandy' and 'quickly' are *not* nouns.

Look at the three **sentences** below. How many nouns can you spot? There is one noun in the first sentence, two in the second sentence, and three in the third.

The nouns are 'lion', 'bird', 'sky', 'flowers', 'trees', and 'garden'.

The lion is roaring.

A bird flies in the sky.

Flowers and trees grow in the garden.

'The', 'a', and 'an'

Nouns often have 'the', 'a', or 'an' in front of them. Try putting 'the' in front of the words in this list. Which words are *not* nouns?

bird

tree

flower

kite

sometimes

pretty

'Sometimes' and 'pretty' are not nouns. You can't say 'the sometimes' or 'the pretty'.

'Antelope' begins with a vowel. 'Giraffe' begins with a consonant.

An <u>a</u>ntelope can run very fast.

A <u>g</u>iraffe is very tall.

We use 'an' if a noun begins with a **vowel**. The vowels are 'a', 'e', 'i', 'o', and 'u'. We use 'a' if a noun begins with a **consonant.** A consonant is any of the other letters.

Singular or plural?

Nouns can be **singular** or **plural**.
A singular noun names one person or
thing. You can put 'a' or 'an' in front of it.

'Sister' and 'brother' are
both singular nouns.

I have a sister and a brother.

Plural nouns name two or more people or things. You usually make plurals by adding 's' to the end of a word.

Dinosaurs were enormous creatures.

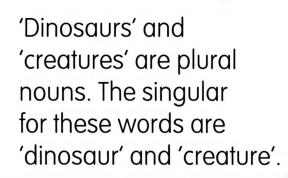

'Dinosaurs' and 'creatures' are plural nouns. The singular for these words are 'dinosaur' and 'creature'.

Common nouns

A common **noun** is a noun that names a type of person or thing. Common nouns can be **singular** or **plural**.

The words in the list are all common nouns.

windows

building

shops

town

street

I like reading books.

Some people look very old.

'Books' and 'people' are common nouns.

Common nouns are used to name general people or things. They are not used to name particular people or things.

Proper nouns

A proper **noun** is the name of a particular person, place, or thing. Proper nouns always begin with a **capital letter**.

Wednesday

New York

David

Market Street

Spain

The nouns in this list are all proper nouns.

Proper nouns usually name things that are one of a kind. You can't put 'the', 'a', or 'an' in front of many proper nouns.

I was born in March.

'March' is a proper noun. It is the name of a particular month.

Collective nouns

A collective **noun** is a noun that describes a group. This can be a group of people, animals, or things.

a herd of cows

a bunch of flowers

In these examples 'herd' and 'bunch' are collective nouns.

In the lists below there are four collective nouns and four groups. Can you match the collective nouns to their groups?

flock	**footballers**
swarm	**sheep**
team	**playing cards**
pack	**bees**

The answers are:
a flock of sheep,
a swarm of bees,
a team of footballers,
a pack of playing cards.

Abstract nouns

Abstract **nouns** are used to describe feelings or qualities. These are things that you cannot see, hear, touch, taste, or smell.

'Happiness' is an abstract noun.

She was filled with happiness.

beauty

sadness

honesty

love

fear

Abstract nouns do not usually have **plurals**.

Look at the list above. All of the nouns in the list are abstract nouns. Can you think of any more?

More plurals

Some **plural nouns** are formed in different ways. If a word ends in 'ss', 'sh', 'ch', or 'x', you need to add 'es'.

The foxes came into the garden.

'Foxes' is plural. The **singular** is 'fox'.

For words that end in 'y', you take away the 'y' and change the ending to 'ies'. But if there is a **vowel** before the 'y', just add 's'. Some plurals, such as 'children' or 'sheep', don't follow rules. You just have to learn them.

In summer, there are lots of flies.

The children are playing outside.

Sheep eat grass.

'Flies' is plural. The singular is 'fly'.
'Children' is plural. The singular is 'child'.
'Sheep' can be both singular and plural!

What is a pronoun?

A **pronoun** is a word that is used to stand for a **noun**. You use a pronoun so that you do not have to use the same noun over and over again.

Anna **strokes** the cat. She **loves** it.

'She' is a pronoun. It stands for 'Anna'. 'It' is a pronoun. It stands for 'the cat'.

> The children **washed** their hands. **Then** they **dried** them.

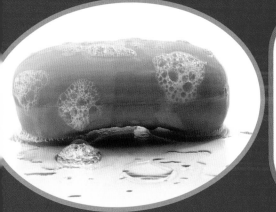

'They' is a plural pronoun. It stands for 'the children'. 'Them' is a plural pronoun. It stands for 'their hands'.

Pronouns can be **singular** or **plural**. In a **sentence**, they stand for singular or plural nouns.

Personal pronouns

A personal **pronoun** stands for a person. It can be the **subject** of a **sentence**. This means it is the person doing the action.

The queen sat on the throne.

or

She sat on the throne.

'She' is a personal pronoun. It stands for 'the queen'. It is the subject of the sentence.

A personal pronoun can also be the **object** of a sentence. This means it is the person the action is being done to. An action or a doing word is called a **verb**.

'Him' stands for 'Josh'. It is the object of the sentence.

The bear chased Josh.

or

The bear chased him.

Possessive pronouns

Some **pronouns** are used to show that something belongs to someone. They are called **possessive** pronouns.

'Mine' is a possessive pronoun. It stands for 'my house'.

Florrie's house is bigger than mine.

This is my hat. Why don't you wear yours?

In this sentence 'yours' is a possessive pronoun. It stands for 'your hat'.

The words 'mine', 'yours', 'ours', 'theirs', 'his', and 'hers' are possessive pronouns. Each one can stand in place of a noun. They show who things belong to.

Find the nouns

How many **nouns** can you think of that fit with the picture below?

Possible answers: elephant; elephants; man; men; woman; women; umbrella; umbrellas; dresses; decorations; sticks; shirts; clothes

Glossary

capital letter an upper-case letter, such as B, F, or Z

consonant a letter that is not a, e, i, o, or u

grammar a set of rules that helps you speak or write clearly

noun a naming word

object the person or thing a verb is being done to

plural meaning more than one person or thing

possessive meaning that something belongs to someone

pronoun a word that stands for a noun

sentence a group of words that makes sense on its own

singular meaning one person or one thing

subject the person or thing that is doing a verb

verb a doing or action word

vowel the letter a, e, i, o, or u

Find out more

Books

Go Further with Grammar, Ruth Thomson (Belitha Press, 2004)

Grammar and Punctuation for School (Homework Helpers), Ladybird (Ladybird Books, 2009)

Grammar Ray series, Andrew Carter (Evans Brothers, 2009)

Websites

www.bbc.co.uk/schools/ks2bitesize/english/spelling_grammar/
Learn about types of words and test yourself on the grammar games.

www.childrensuniversity.manchester.ac.uk/interactives/literacy/
wordclasses/nouns.asp
Find out more about nouns and try a noun game and quiz.

Index